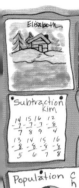

Teacher, You're an A+

Text by Cheryl Kirking

Paintings by Heidi Satterberg

HARVEST HOUSE PUBLISHERS

EUGENE, OREGON

ENGLISH

HISTORY

Teacher, You're an A+

Text Copyright © 2003 by Cheryl Kirking
Published by Harvest House Publishers
Eugene, Oregon 97402

Published in association with the literary agency of Alive Communications, Inc., 7680 Goddard Street, Suite 200, Colorado Springs, CO 80920.

Libraray of Congress Cataloging-in-Publication Data

Kirking, Cheryl, 1959-
    Teacher, you're an A+ / text by Cheryl Kirking ; artwork by Heidi Satterberg.
        p. cm.
    ISBN 0-7369-0892-7
  1. Teachers—Religious life—Anecdotes. I. Title: Teacher, you're an A plus.
II. Satterberg, Heidi. III. Title.
    BV4596.T43 K57 2003
    371.1—dc21

                                                    2002011138

Cheryl Kirking is a speaker, songwriter, and author. A former teacher, she frequently keynotes at conferences for educators and parents. To correspond with her, please contact Ripples of Encouragement, P.O. Box 525, Lake Mills, WI 53551 or www.cherylkirking.com

Artwork designs by Heidi Satterberg are reproduced under license from ©Arts Uniq'®, Inc., Cookeville, TN and may not be reproduced without permission. For more information regarding art prints featured in this book, please contact: Arts Uniq', P.O. Box 3085, Cookeville, TN 38502, 1.800.223.5020.

Design and production by Garborg Design Works, Minneapolis, Minnesota

All quotes, stories, and poems without attribution are the original works of the author.

Harvest House Publishers has made every effort to trace the ownership of all quotes. In the event of a question arising from the use of a quote, we regret any error made and will be pleased to make the necessary correction in future editions of this book.

Printed in China

03 04 05 06 07 08 09 10 / IM / 10 9 8 7 6 5 4 3 2 1

Presented to

Our Wee Maid,
Rachel, with fondest
love from Mum and Dad
xxx x♡

because you're an A+!

A teacher affects eternity;
she can never tell where her influence stops.

HENRY ADAMS

Heidi Satterberg ©

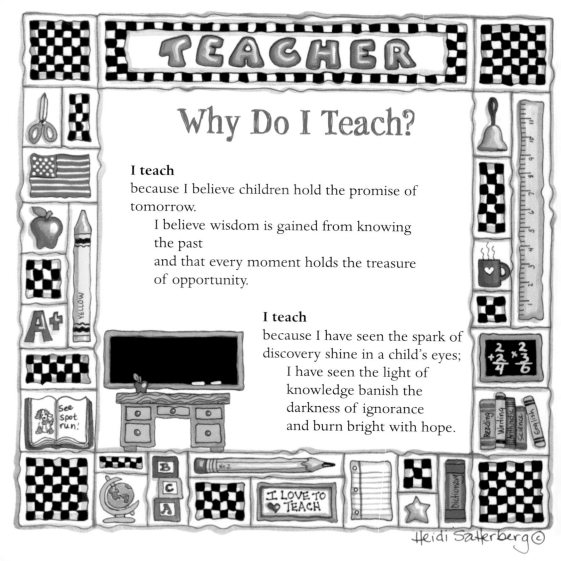

TEACHER

Why Do I Teach?

I teach
because I believe children hold the promise of
tomorrow.
I believe wisdom is gained from knowing
the past
and that every moment holds the treasure
of opportunity.

I teach
because I have seen the spark of
discovery shine in a child's eyes;
I have seen the light of
knowledge banish the
darkness of ignorance
and burn bright with hope.

Heidi Satterberg ©

I teach
because I know the difference one individual can make
through a single act of kindness or encouragement.

I teach
because I celebrate the potential of each child.

I teach
because I delight in learning,
and every day I teach

I learn.

CHERYL KIRKING

5

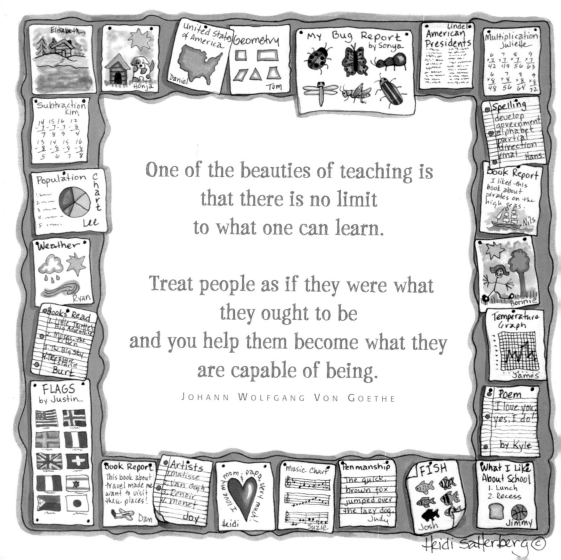

One of the beauties of teaching is
that there is no limit
to what one can learn.

Treat people as if they were what
they ought to be
and you help them become what they
are capable of being.

JOHANN WOLFGANG VON GOETHE

A Teacher
Learns a Lesson

I was just 22 when I landed my first teaching job at a large high school. Fresh out of college, I was anxious to teach, but found that I still had a lot of learning to do.

I learned many things that first year, but the greatest lesson came from John, a tall, gangly sophomore in my fifth-hour American studies class. On the first day of class, John interrupted me frequently with one-liners and complained loudly about how uncomfortable the desks were for his awkward, 6-foot, 3-inch frame. He wasn't malicious, just pesky. I knew I was going to have to win him over, or it would be a long year indeed. I could see that he not only needed a lot of attention but had other needs as well: His shoes had holes in them, and his clothes were obviously well worn.

The next day I informed John that his new seat was

front row, center, where he could stretch out his long legs…under the condition that he pull his size 14 feet back whenever I needed to walk by.

"Admit it, Miss Kirking, you just want me closer to your desk because I'm your favorite student!" he joked.

"John, you are so smart…you saw right through my little ploy!" I joked back.

John seemed content with the arrangement, and I could tell that he tried very hard to keep his outbursts to a minimum. Whenever he was too loud or began to interrupt, an admonishing glance was all it took for him to bring his mouth under control. He was usually the first to class, which met right after lunch. He would saunter in, drop his books loudly on his desk, and announce, "Miss Kirking, your favorite student has arrived!"

"Thank you, John," I would reply with a bow, "for gracing us yet another day with your presence!"

Near the end of the first semester, I was having a particularly frustrating day. I had a terrible head cold and was grumpy and tired. The students were complaining about the upcoming final exam, and I was having trouble getting everyone to quiet down. When I finally got everyone's attention, I warned the students, "I am passing out your assignment. I want you to get to work immediately and be quiet—I don't want to hear one more word!"

"How about two more words?" John quipped.

"John!" I snapped, *"Shut up!"* John winced as if I had slapped him. His cheeks and ears flushed red, and the hurt in his eyes made me immediately regret my harsh words.

I was so ashamed. I had been raised not to use the words "shut up." I couldn't blame it on the unruly students or my head cold or John. I had blown it—and it was my responsibility to fix the situation somehow. How could I have been so disrespectful? As the sullen students worked silently on their assignments, I wondered what I

should do. I feared I had broken the trust John and I had established.

"John," I said, loudly enough for the rest of the class to hear, "I didn't show you much respect today. I am really sorry."

Still looking stunned, John shrugged and answered softly, "It's okay."

Finally the bell rang, and the class shuffled out. John lingered behind and slowly approached my desk.

"I can't believe you said that to me," he remarked incredulously.

"I know, John. I shouldn't have told you to shut up," I said.

"No," he replied, "not that you told me to shut up. I can't believe that you said you were sorry. That's pretty cool." He gave me a little grin as he turned to leave.

John helped me learn one of my most important lessons as an educator: Respect and kindness are my most important tools.

Kindness strengthens
itself by calling forth
answering kindness.
Hence it is the furthest
reaching and most
effective of all forces.

ALBERT SCHWEITZER

Heidi Satterberg ©

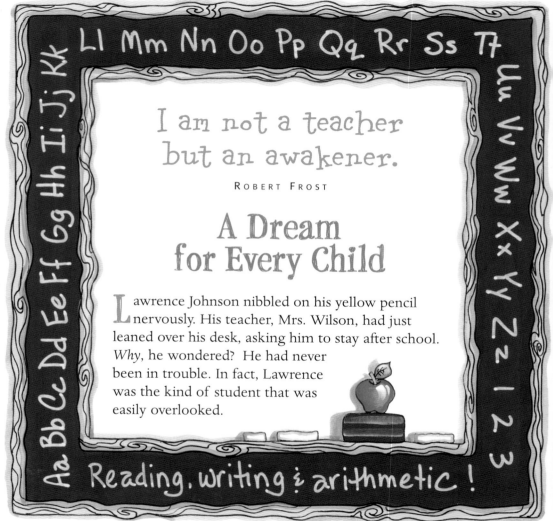

> I am not a teacher
> but an awakener.
>
> ROBERT FROST

A Dream for Every Child

Lawrence Johnson nibbled on his yellow pencil nervously. His teacher, Mrs. Wilson, had just leaned over his desk, asking him to stay after school. *Why*, he wondered? He had never been in trouble. In fact, Lawrence was the kind of student that was easily overlooked.

Heidi Satterberg ©

Academically, he was quite average. Painfully shy and awkward, he had no close friends, but that was fine with him. He had learned last year in fourth grade that if he could just try to be invisible, he wouldn't get picked on by anyone, or draw attention to himself when he stumbled over his feet, which seemed too big for his slight frame.

The dismissal bell rang, and Lawrence stayed behind as the other students filed out. He hoped Mrs. Wilson wouldn't keep him after school long—his grandmother counted the minutes until he got home every day.

Mrs. Wilson motioned for Lawrence to sit in the chair by her desk. "Lawrence," she began in her kind voice, "in celebration of Dr. Martin Luther King's birthday we'll be having a special class program later this month. We'll be inviting parents and grandparents to attend. I'd like you to read Dr. King's famous speech, 'I Have a Dream.' I think you will do an excellent job." She placed the stapled pages of the speech in his hands.

"Me?" Lawrence shifted nervously from one foot to the other

while pushing his glasses onto the bridge of his nose. The speech was three pages long! "I can't," he stammered. "Not the whole thing. Not in front of everybody!"

"I know you can, Lawrence. Here's a note for your grandmother, telling her that you'll be staying after school tomorrow, so we can watch a videotape of Dr. King giving the speech. Then you can practice it with me."

Lawrence nodded quietly. What else could he do?

The next day after school Lawrence and Mrs. Wilson watched the video of Dr. King, pausing the tape after each paragraph to discuss the meaning of the words. Lawrence understood these were powerful words he would be reading. He felt privileged… and very, very nervous.

Over the next two weeks, Mrs. Wilson's students wrote reports about the great civil rights leader and hung them

14

around the classroom. They wrote and practiced a skit in which each student played a part. They learned two songs. The day before their program they had a dress rehearsal. But when it came time to read his speech, Lawrence whispered to his teacher, "Mrs. Wilson, please don't make me do it in front of the class. Please? I'll be ready tomorrow. I promise."

Mrs. Wilson paused. Her common sense told her that she needed to make Lawrence practice in front of the group. But she listened to her instinct, which said, *"Wait. Give him time."*

The next morning, parents, grandparents, and even the principal came and sat in folding chairs by the students' desks. Lawrence's grandmother arrived in her best flowered dress and sat in the chair next to his desk in the last row.

The students shared their skit and songs, then Janessa introduced Lawrence: "This speech was delivered by Dr. Martin Luther King, Jr., on the steps of the Lincoln Memorial in Washington D.C. on August 28, 1963. Today this famous speech will be read by Lawrence Johnson."

Lawrence walked slowly to the front of the room; his feet felt like bricks. He felt choked by the tie and starched white shirt his grandmother made him wear. He glanced briefly at the audience, swallowed hard, and read:

Five score years ago, a great American, in whose symbolic shadow we stand, signed the Emancipation Proclamation. This momentous decree came as a great beacon light of hope to millions of Negro slaves who had been seared in the flames of withering injustice...

Lawrence stared at the words, forcing himself to keep reading, willing his voice to stop shaking. Three paragraphs, four, five…

We must forever conduct our struggle on the high plane of dignity and discipline. We must not allow our creative protest to degenerate into physical violence…

Gradually, with each paragraph, Lawrence's voice grew stronger. He looked up from the pages he held. He didn't need to read the

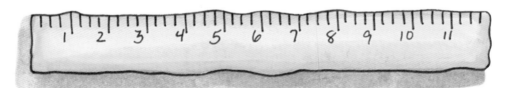

speech. He knew it by heart. He *felt* it by heart. He was strong, empowered by a hero's words.

I have a dream that one day this nation will rise up and live out the true meaning of its creed: "We hold these truths to be self-evident: that all men are created equal." ...I have a dream that my four children will one day live in a nation where they will not be judged by the color of their skin but by the content of their character.

Lawrence spoke fervently, standing tall, much taller than he had just minutes before. His eyes were bright and his voice passionate as he concluded with the famous words:

When we let freedom ring, when we let it ring from

every village and every hamlet, from every state and every city, we will be able to speed up that day when all of God's children, black men and white men, Jews and Gentiles, Protestants and Catholics, will be able to join hands and sing in the words of the old Negro spiritual, "Free at last! Free at last! Thank God Almighty, we are free at last!"

There was a reverent hush in the classroom. His grandmother dabbed at her round brown cheeks with her hanky. The principal led the applause as he stood and walked to the front of the classroom to shake Lawrence's hand.

Sixteen more students would give Dr. King's speech in the remaining years that Mrs. Wilson taught fifth grade at Central Elementary, and she chose each speaker with

great consideration. Mrs. Wilson was a talent scout. Her goal was to help each student discover a hidden gift during their fifth-grade year. Reading Dr. King's famous speech was just one of many tools she used to unlock her students' inner talents, guiding them toward their strengths. And for many, their year with Mrs. Wilson was a turning point as it was for Lawrence, who discovered the voice of the strong man he would one day become.

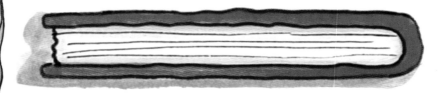

Intelligence plus character—that is the goal of true education.

MARTIN LUTHER KING, JR.

Reading, writing & arithmetic!

Heidi Satterberg ©

What do you like about your teacher?

Answers from elementary school children

When I'm done with my work, she lets me get up and go to the work stations if I'm good and quiet. This is good for me so I don't get bored and I stay out of trouble.

BEN, 6

She will let us play a game sometimes when we're too full of the wiggles.

JULIANA, 7

She lets us write in chocolate pudding on our desks!

JOE, 6

She talks to me when I'm sad.

JONATHON, 8

22

She doesn't punish the whole class when only two boys are naughty.

AIMEE, 8

He has a kind way of speaking.

LANE, 7

I like it how she smells good and her eyelashes.

SARA, 6

She takes us on walks and tells us what to look for.

SAM, 8

She talks to us about her pets and things she does at her home.

AIMEE, 8

He lets us earn points for goodness.

RENEE, 7

Like many other values our children get from us, compassion is more likely to be caught than taught.

FRED ROGERS

23

Play is often talked about as if it were a relief from serious learning, but for children play is serious learning. Play is really the work of childhood.

FRED ROGERS

Heidi Satterberg ©

To show a child what once delighted you, to find the child's delight added to your own...this is happiness.

J.B. PRIESTLY

Excuses, Excuses

My husband is known as a fair but strict teacher. Tall, with black hair, neatly trimmed beard, and glasses, he presents quite a serious image. However, he allows

Heidi Satterberg©

his dry sense of humor to break through. For example, he quietly reminds his students that they'll need to pass his required classes in order to graduate. Posted above his classroom clock is a small, handwritten sign which reads:

"Time passes...will you?"

For geography class, his sophomore students must complete a detailed map of Europe and then use it as a study guide for a major quiz. On the day of the quiz, when the map was to be handed in for credit, Jason approached my husband's desk with trepidation. "Mr. Kilker," he said haltingly, "I don't have my map."

My husband silently waited for an explanation.

"You see," Jason explained, blushing, "last night I was studying in the living room for today's quiz and I got up to get a drink of water. When I came back my map was gone!"

To invent you need a good imagination and a pile of junk.

THOMAS EDISON

RED

> There are no secrets to success. It is the result of preparation, hard work, and learning from failure.
>
> COLIN POWELL

My husband looked dubious.

"Well, my dad was stompin' and hollerin' about the dog chewin' up everything, and he was throwing little bits of paper into the fire! He didn't know it was my map!" Jason's ears flamed bright red with embarrassment. "This is all I could save," he mumbled miserably, as he dug three tiny chewed bits of map out of his jeans pocket and sheepishly laid them out on the desk.

A grin broke across my husband's stern face as Jason pleaded, "You gotta believe me…the dog really *did* eat my homework!"

Book Report
This book about travel made me want to visit these places!
✈ Dan

• Artists
1. Matisse
2. Van Gogh
3. Renoir
4. Monet
Joy

A Good Teacher...
Answers from middle school students

Likes teaching kids our age.
AMBER, 13

Doesn't play favorites.
ALEXANDER, 14

Lets you have fun, but knows how to get the class back under control.
LENA, 13

Will stay after school if you need help or to talk.
KALEE, 13

READING WRITING ARITHMETIC SCIENCE HISTORY

The first pencils were string-wrapped pieces of graphite.
The average adult has about 2,800 square inches of skin.
Halley's Comet appears about every 76 years.
A symphony is music written for an orchestra.

Learn something new every day !!!

The highest function
of the teacher consists
not so much in imparting
knowledge as in
stimulating the pupil
in its love and pursuit.

HENRI FREDERIC AMIEL

A fly beats its wings about 190 times a second.
"Happy Birthday" was written by the Hill sisters in 1893.
Pine cones open in good weather, close before storms.
Alaska is the largest U.S. state, Rhode Island the smallest.

U.S. women were given the right to vote in 1920.
In Roman numerals, X=10, L=50, C=100, D=500, M=1000.
Mother's Day is observed the second Sunday in May.
Benjamin Franklin's portrait is on the U.S. 100 dollar bill.

Most butterflies fly by day, moths by night.
"Hippopotamus" means "river horse."
Neil Armstrong walked on the moon in 1969.
The Grand Canyon is 277 miles long.

Heidi Satterberg ©

approached my desk. "Teacher, I want you to know, thanks to you my family had the best Christmas ever."

Surprised at his unexpected statement, I asked, "How did I help?"

"Well, my father hurt his back where he works. Money has been pretty scarce. I took home that wreath you showed us how to make. We was all sitting around the kitchen table looking it over. Mother said she thought we ought to be able to sell some wreaths to get Christmas money. She said 'Go get those extra coat hangers in the closets.' My father knew there was some wire in the shop almost like what we used and we had plenty of fir brush growing on our land. Us five kids all went off to gather up supplies. I showed them how to cut the brush and wire it to the coat hanger ring.

"We made fifty wreaths and tied them on top of the station wagon. Mother found enough stuff to decorate one real pretty. All of us climbed into the car and headed for Augusta. We parked in that big parking lot at the mall and put up our cardboard

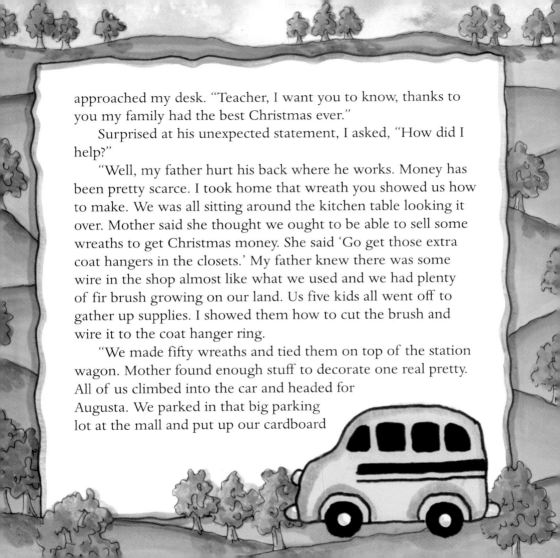

sign. We sold the first one in nothing flat! Mother took that money and went into the store and bought decorations. We sold every wreath as fast as she and I could decorate them. We got five whole dollars a piece for the rest of 'em!

"Well, we divvied up the money between us and went shopping. Boy, it was fun to see my brothers and sisters learning to make those wreaths and then shopping with the money they got for selling them.

"My folks wanted me to say thanks, Teacher. You really helped us out."

I thanked him and patted him on the back as I turned away so he wouldn't see my tears. My joy in teaching had come back to me full circle—like the circle of those wreaths.

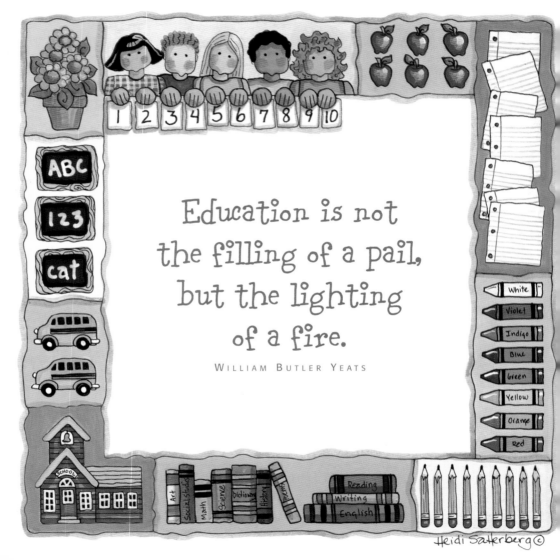

Education is not the filling of a pail, but the lighting of a fire.

WILLIAM BUTLER YEATS

Top Ten Signs You Teach Young Children

10. As you head out the door on a shopping trip, you ask your friends: "Does anyone have to go to the bathroom before we leave? Are you *sure*?"

9. When your mother broke her arm and you needed to tie her shoes, you double-knotted the laces.

Heidi Satterberg©

8. You grab the hands of anyone nearby as you cross the street and refuse to let go until you reach the other side.

7. You tuck tissues in the hands of runny-nosed strangers.

6. While in the check-out line at the grocery store, you say to the people behind you, "I like the way you are waiting patiently."

5. You then tell the grocery bagger, "I like the way you packed the groceries so neatly!"

4. You holler "Watch your fingers!" any time you close a door.

3. Instead of inviting your neighbor in for coffee, you ask if she'd "like to come for snack-time?"

2. When your dinner partner returns from the restroom, you ask, "Did you wash your hands?"

1. When a man in your pew whispers during church, you ask if he "has something to share with the whole group?"

The most potent of all indirect influences in the development of our citizenry is the influence of a good teacher.

ARMOND J. GERSON

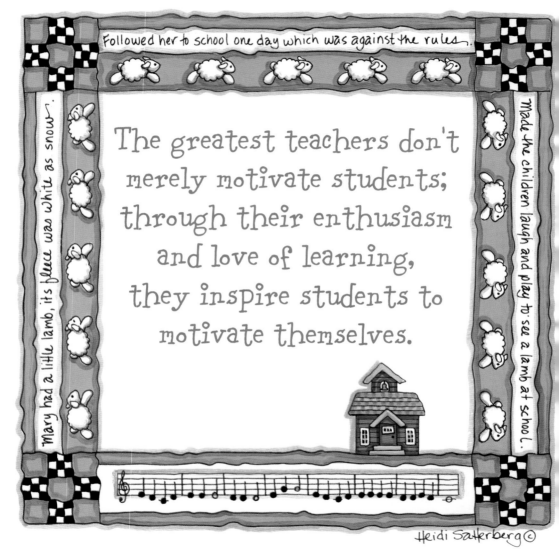

Give My Regards

Carnegie Hall seems like a long way from a small dairy farm in rural Wisconsin. But Tom Wopat began his journey to its stage with the encouragement of his high school chorus teacher.

"I guess I've been singing all my life," says the star of Broadway and television. "I even sang on the tractor as I worked on our farm growing up. But I never considered music as a career until my chorus teacher, Don Roebuck, saw some talent in me.

"Don loved the stage and had been in a number of stage productions himself. He was a colorful individual—sort of a rebel in the education world, I guess you could say—with an unruly mop of hair to match his spirited personality. When he launched into a new project, like the annual high school musical, he

> The dream begins most of the time with a teacher who believes in you, who tugs and pushes, and leads you on to the next plateau, sometimes poking you with a sharp stick called "truth."
>
> DAN RATHER

put his whole heart into it, and his students couldn't help but catch his enthusiasm.

"Tom," Mr. Roebuck would say, "there's a future for you on the stage. Go after it."

And Tom did. He performed in campus productions and summer stock, which led him to New York where he starred in on- and off-Broadway shows. During a trip to the West Coast, he auditioned for and won the role of Luke Duke, and for seven seasons *The Dukes of Hazzard* was a popular television phenom-enon. For Wopat, it provided both stardom and an education. During the show's span, Wopat also continued to develop his musical talents, writing songs and touring the country with his band. But his passion has always been the stage, where Tom ultimately returned.

"I suppose just about every singer dreams of singing at Carnegie Hall, and in 1997 that dream came true for me. I was invited to sing Broadway songs, accompanied by the Cincinnati Symphony Orchestra. Many of my hometown friends would be there for my first Carnegie Hall appearance. A number of them, like myself, went into the performing arts as a result of Mr. Roebuck's encouragement. The big night wouldn't be complete without Don. I called him and he told me he wouldn't miss it for the world. So I flew him to New York and made sure he had a great box seat."

It was the trip of a lifetime for the retired music teacher, who was thrilled to see a number of his favorite students. It was a

Made the children laugh and play to see a lamb at school.

well-timed reunion, as the beloved teacher passed away unexpectedly later that year.

"After a few songs, as I was about to sing Andrew Lloyd Webber's 'Memory' from the musical *Cats*, I announced that I wanted to dedicate it to someone very special. I tell you, it was an emotional moment as Don stood, his face flushed bright red with pride, wreathed with a halo of silver hair. It was a privilege to be able to put the spotlight on him, the man who had gotten me seriously interested in singing in the first place. The applause from the audience was long and heartfelt, and—in some small way— expressed my gratitude to my friend, my mentor, my teacher."

The sign of a great teacher is that the accomplishments of his students exceed his own.

ARISTOTLE

A Good Teacher...

Answers from high school students

Has the students' respect and treats every student with respect.

KEENAN, 16

Has a clue what our world is like.

JENNA, 15

Will keep YOU on task, but let YOU wander off a bit if the DISCUSSION is really good.

JESS, 18

Makes the subject interesting by getting excited about it.

MATT, 14

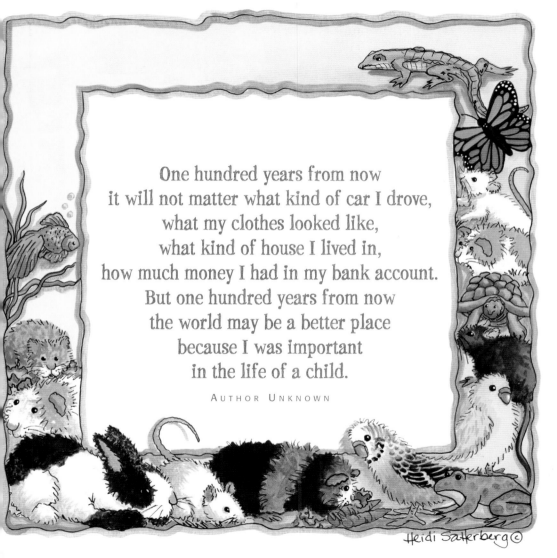

One hundred years from now
it will not matter what kind of car I drove,
what my clothes looked like,
what kind of house I lived in,
how much money I had in my bank account.
But one hundred years from now
the world may be a better place
because I was important
in the life of a child.

AUTHOR UNKNOWN

Heidi Satterberg©

The fine art of teaching is to guide the growth of the learner so that after each experience he is one step closer to maturity.

OVID F. PARODY

Over the Rainbow

"Don't forget," Mrs. VandeBerg reminded, "tomorrow we'll have tryouts for our class play. Anyone interested in auditioning for a speaking part may pick up a script from my desk to take home. The parts are described at the top of the first page."

The dismissal bell rang and I reached for a script through the tangle of students gathered around Mrs. VandeBerg's desk. The stapled pages were still slightly damp and fragrant of mimeograph fluid. *The Wizard of Oz*! I eagerly skimmed the cast list: *Dorothy: a Kansas farm girl seeking adventure. Scarecrow: a friendly scarecrow seeking a brain.*

> The young do not know enough to be prudent, and therefore they attempt the impossible and achieve it, generation after generation.
>
> PEARL S. BUCK

Tin Man, Lion, Auntie Em…all the familiar parts of my favorite movie were listed.

As the students poured out of the school doors, a group of fifth-grade girls from my classroom chattered excitedly about who might get the part of Dorothy.

"Susan will probably get the part. She has long brown hair," Debby said.

"But Dorothy doesn't have to have dark hair," Brenda replied. "I think Jill should be Dorothy."

Other names were tossed about, but mine wasn't among them. With my short pixie cut, skinny legs, and blue cat-eye glasses, I knew I didn't stand a chance.

Still, I was excited at the prospect of being in the play. Settling into my seat on the bus, I tried to look casual as I poured over the script again. I didn't want anyone to see how badly I wanted a part. As the bus bounced along, I studied the cast list again, reading the description of each role until I reached the bottom of the list—*Toto: Dorothy's little dog.* Flipping through the pages, I noticed Toto's part repeated the same one-word line several times: *"Woof."* I could play that part!

The next day I wore my black corduroy jumper and black tights, hoping to look as Toto-like as possible. Mid-morning break finally came, and Mrs. VandeBerg announced auditions would begin, starting at the end of the cast list. "Who would like to read for the

part of Toto?" she asked. I rose eagerly, glad to see I was the only one trying out. Then Kathy stepped forward. My heart sank. Petite and pretty with dark curls, she'd make the perfect Toto! I *woofed* my best, but Mrs. VandeBerg announced that Kathy would be Toto. Although she made a very cute Toto, I thought I had a more convincing bark!

Next came tryouts for the Guard at the Wizard's Door. Even though it was a boy's part, I tried. I read for the part of Auntie Em, the Good Witch, and the Bad Witch. I danced like the Scarecrow, rattled like the Tin Man, and roared my best like the Lion. But after each attempt, I returned to my desk without a part.

"All those interested in trying out for Dorothy, please come forward." Seven girls walked to the front of

the room. I slowly rose from my desk to join them, even though I knew it was not likely that I would get the coveted lead role. I couldn't even win the part of the dog!

After we had each read, Mrs. VandeBerg leaned over her desk, her hands folded delicately. "Girls, you all read very well. But I can only choose one girl, and Dorothy will be played by…Cheryl."

Education is the ability to meet life's expectations.

DR. JOHN G. HIBBIN

I couldn't believe it! I was thrilled but a bit embarrassed. I thought surely some of the other girls would resent me. However, as I raised my eyes to meet theirs, I didn't see

any resentment at all. Naturally, some were disappointed, but they listened intently and seemed to understand as Mrs. VandeBerg explained: "Cheryl showed us all that you should never give up. *The Wizard of Oz* is a play about going on, even when it may be hard to do...yet also learning to be content with what you have in the meantime."

Mrs. VandeBerg's lesson was not lost. It is a lesson I have remembered many times in my life—to keep reaching for my dreams, yet strive to be content along the way.

And "Over the Rainbow" is still my favorite song.

Epilogue: While preparing this book, I tracked down and called Mrs. VandeBerg. It had been 32 years since we spoke, and we had a wonderful time reminiscing. I highly recommend contacting a favorite past teacher! Who are you going to call?

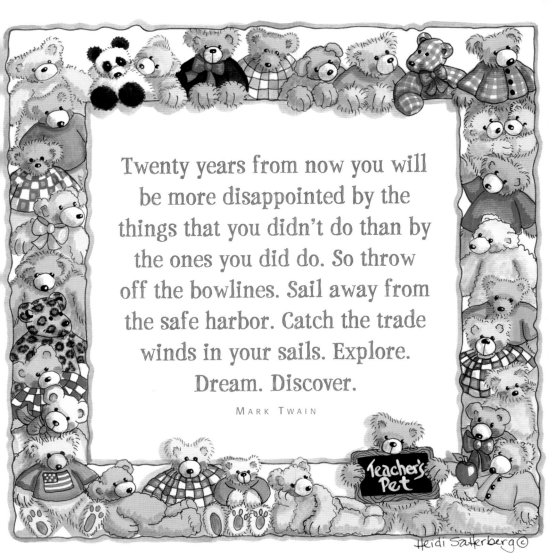

Twenty years from now you will be more disappointed by the things that you didn't do than by the ones you did do. So throw off the bowlines. Sail away from the safe harbor. Catch the trade winds in your sails. Explore. Dream. Discover.

MARK TWAIN

Teacher's Pet

Heidi Satterberg©

Wanted: The Perfect Teacher

Library books due tomorrow

There's a teaching position open—
It shouldn't be hard to fill;
Here are a few qualifications
For one who might fit the bill:

He must be old and dignified,
And preferably young and fun;
She must be stylish, with lots of clothes,
Yet grandmotherly, with hair in a bun.

He must have thirty years experience
And at least a master's degree,
And come fresh out of college
With lots of energy.

Heidi Satterberg©

She mustn't require many supplies
And will work for minimal pay;
He must never get a cold or flu
Or miss a single day.

She must be very easy-going
But as strict as strict can be;
He must not give out homework
Yet cover the textbook thoroughly.

She must discipline the students
Without ever making them mad,
And *never* upset a parent—
(That's always very bad.)

He mustn't push the kids too hard
Yet his tests should all be essay;
He must make sure that no one fails them,
And have them corrected by the next day.

His bulletin boards must be clever—
A delight to the eye and mind.
Her lesson plans must be perfect
With lengthy objectives defined.

She must account for her paper usage.
His desk should always be neat.
She must not waste time on frivolous things,
But give out lots of treats.

She must prepare the students completely,
While making sure they are not stressed,
When they have to sit for hours
Taking long standardized tests.

He should have a well-rounded life
For it's important to be that way,
But take phone calls and attend meetings
At any time of the day.

This list rings with bits of truth
Although it may seem in jest,
But one thing is for certain—
Teacher, you're the best!

In spite of many challenges
You somehow find a way
To touch the future, one child at a time,
By caring every day.

CHERYL KIRKING

The invariable mark of wisdom is to see the miraculous in the common.

RALPH WALDO EMERSON

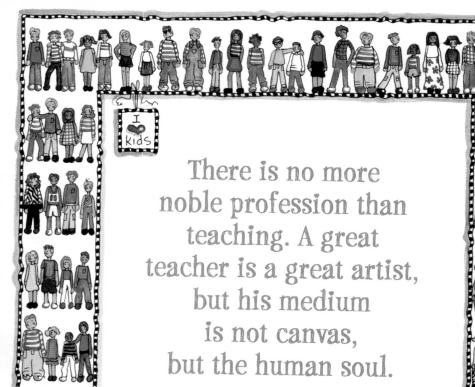

There is no more
noble profession than
teaching. A great
teacher is a great artist,
but his medium
is not canvas,
but the human soul.

AUTHOR UNKNOWN

Heidi Satterberg©